FUCHSIA

DISCARDED

DISCARDED

African POETRY BOOK SERIES

Series editor: Kwame Dawes

EDITORIAL BOARD

Kwame Dawes, University
of Nebraska-Lincoln

Chris Abani, University of
California, Riverside

Matthew Shenoda, Columbia
College, Chicago

Gabeba Baderoon, Pennsylvania
State University

John Keene, Rutgers University

Bernardine Evaristo, Brunel
University and UEA-*Guardian*

ADVISORY BOARD

Laura Sillerman

Glenna Luschei

Sulaiman Adebowale

Elizabeth Alexander

Russell Goings

FUCHSIA

Mahtem Shiferraw

Foreword by Kwame Dawes

University of Nebraska Press / Lincoln and London

© 2016 by the Board of Regents of
the University of Nebraska

Acknowledgments for the use of copyrighted
material appear on page xix, which constitutes
an extension of the copyright page.

All rights reserved
Manufactured in the United States of America
⊛

The African Poetry Series has been
made possible through the generosity
of philanthropists Laura and Robert
F. X. Sillerman, whose contributions have
facilitated the establishment and operation
of the African Poetry Book Fund.

Library of Congress
Cataloging-in-Publication Data
Shiferraw, Mahtem.
[Poems. Selections]
Fushsia / Mahtem Shiferraw;
foreword by Kwame Dawes.
pages   cm.—(African poetry book series)
ISBN 978-0-8032-8556-9 (pbk.: alk. paper)
ISBN 978-0-8032-8590-3 (pdf)
I. Dawes, Kwame Senu Neville, 1962– II. Title.
PS3619.H5435A6 2016
811'.6—dc23
2015032076

Set in Garamond Premier by L. Auten.

CONTENTS

FOREWORD

Kwame Dawes

I have found the note that makes my voice call
I have swallowed emptiness, to be full
I have seen color everywhere
— Matthew Shenoda, *Tahrir Suite*

It is exciting to see a poet working intensely at precision of language to
capture the most difficult things for language to capture—sound is one,
and, of course, color. Indeed, if one wanted to witness what it may well be
like to have a poet enact the condition of someone suffering from synes-
thesia, Mahtem Shiferraw would be a prime case study. Again and again,
colors are loaded with rich and complex meaning. This collection offers
multiple versions of blood as color—proposing different shades for the
blood of different animals. In the poem "Synesthesia" the chemistry of
this condition is enacted richly, and we see a poetic formula at work. Here
is what she does with brown—note the range, the emotional and physical
range of this telling:

Brown is the anomalous texture of curtains from my
childhood. Brown is also the parched wood
of a small coffee grinder my mother used. Brown as in
the intimate angles of sharply cut *ambasha* my grandmother

made, flour and water, lemon skin and cinnamon shreds, the
dark heads of raisins, while on a cargo plane back to Ethiopia,
the tired eyes of war victims and their slow recovery. Brown
is also the color of my skin, but I didn't know it then.

These efforts remind us of just how much we rely on core poetic devices
to engage the world, and somehow to replicate it. The effort to so employ
language in the most talented poets produces a combination of surprise,
delight, and admiration in those of us who value the uses of language and
who appreciate the limitations of language. Here is Shiferraw's splendid
evocation of color in the title poem, "Fuchsia," which opens her collection:

If you ask how to say "burgundy" in Tigrinya, you will be told
it's the color of sheep blood, without the musty smell
of death attached to it. It's also the color of my hair, dipped
in fire. And the greasy texture of clotted arteries, and the folding
skin of pineapple lilies, and the sagging insides of decaying roses,
and the butterfly leaves of blooming perennials, and spongy
strawberries drowning in wine.

In this small sequence we observe the way she invents the practices of a
culture through a seamless evocation of the public — the communal — and
the private. We trust that it is true that a Tigrinya speaker would reach for
this quite specific language that combines the visual and the olfactory to
describe the color "burgundy" — a word, in English, that clearly has similar
properties of sight and scent. But we truly only have to trust Shiferraw's
account of it in the way that we trust her private invention, which engages
the surreal without fanfare or alarm: "the color of my hair, dipped / in
fire." From there, the rest is splendid evocation — how the reach for color
is the reach for mood, for culture, for the texture of sentiment and experi-
ence culminating in this marvelous return to "burgundy" — this time, the
"spongy / strawberries drowning in wine." This is a study of poetic obsession,
and what we get is the indisputable evidence that beyond any desire to say
something, to communicate some of the complexity of the world, some

polemical or political idea, there is in Shiferraw a desire to challenge her skills as a poet, to capture, through the limitations of language, the infinite possibilities of our universe.

And so when she tackles the color "fuchsia," we understand that Shiferraw is reaching for something wonderfully elusive — memory and its fictive and inventive possibilities. This passage of verse is as good an introduction to Shiferraw's poetry as anything she has written because it is constantly reaching, and even its failings (how the forgotten is actually the remembered, and how there is no language to achieve both remembering and forgetting in the same instant) are remarkable in what they achieve:

And then, you ask, what is fuchsia — and there's a faint smile,
a sudden remembrance, an afterthought in hiding, forgotten smells
of wild flowers and days spent in hiding, in disarray. And mulberry
daisies carried by phosphorescent winds into the warm skin of sleeping
bodies; moments spent between here and there, pockets of emptiness —
without sound, without reckoning.

Shiferraw's collection seeks to map landscapes of memory and geography — the two elements overlapping in dynamic ways. Her world is palpable and rich with physical detail. Structured around the idea of movement, these poems invite us into her various spaces of "home" beginning with "Origins & Intersections," a poem that transports us in time and geography, through ancient East Africa with its colorful markets and medieval edifices, and farther into the Dahlak shrublands where cactus fruit bloom, into Godaif where women watch their sons slaughtered through small holes in their walls, and into the network of waterways related to the Nile basin, to Lake Tana, where the mysteries of the river are celebrated:

And beneath it all, something sleeps, damp and forgotten
and cavernous in its roar — only those who drink its swelling
waters can hear it, and recount its secrets.
("Something Sleeps in the Mud Beds of the Nile")

Shiferraw and her various characters describe Asmara as the dead city, Massawa as the bombed city remembered for the screams of the wounded, Karen as a city that produces the wave of merchants, the village of Gejeret as a shelter for a guerilla uncle, and the mountains of Jubba as a place where some of the lost uncles have finally settled. The Red Sea is part of her mother's imagined world, and ultimately, these are places Shiferraw invokes as part of her history, both her personal history and the history of her parents who have fled from these memories.

Thus when the poet arrives in America ("While Weeping [Broadway & 5th]") — another place of migration, of arrivals and departures (one assumes to be Los Angeles, which she later describes as a "monster") — memory has a context, and she understands herself to have belonged somewhere before arriving in this new place. But in this place, memory proves to be malleable and at risk. One has the sense that the collecting of stories, the stirring of memory, the invention, if you will, of narratives of remembrance, represent a desperate attempt to fight back the encroachment of anomie:

You must have forgotten yourself here,
            because   I have no recollection
                                    of the aftermath.
Something is fading from
the corners, cascading itself on
                        corroded, corrupted
                            walls. Weeping
                                walls. Walls with
                                cloudless
graffiti knifed in them.

It is not entirely clear who the "you" might be since this person is offered in some counter distinction to the "I" speaker. But this figure recurs throughout, and increasingly, it appears that the poet may well be in constant dialogue with her useful id or alter ego. But this figure, in these poems, seeks to resolve a series of troubled questions about home and place and even identity. She lists her identities all over the collection, whether Ethiopian, or Eritrean, or African, or African American, or other, and then concludes in a manner that presents a poignant sense of alienation, even as it invokes a sense of community, a shared sense of belonging ("nomads like me"):

I don't know how to fit, adjust myself within new boundaries —
nomads like me, have no place as home, no way of belonging.
("Talks about Race")

Africa, as a site of defining and making, is, at once, a place of beauty and evocative delights, even while it is a place of mystery, haunting and palpable instability, and threat. In so many poems, all these elements come together. Even when the memory has been transformed by the telling into a kind of myth ("These dreams are not real"), it is distilled into impulses of foreboding and disquiet as in "Sleeping with Hyenas" or "She says they come at night...":

Firstborn sons were killed on a quiet night,
like any other.

I say diligent thieves get only
what they came for.

She says they do.
("She says they come at night . . .")

Shiferraw finds sources of comfort in her willingness to confront both memory and the harrowing of the presence. In "Dialectics of Death" what we find is not a cerebral exploration of death and its implications, but a dogged, almost irritating desire to ask the hard questions ("When would you like to die?" "If you knew, would you hide?" "Old age, great illness, to die in your sleep?") The answers are illuminating—are rich with the stories of friends, family, and the poet herself trying to make sense of these questions without, sometimes, even bothering to answer them. Sometimes the stories are disturbing, like the image of Mayumi's father, hanged, body lacerated, a single eye gouged out and one left alone, and Mayumi who is still asking the question — "Have you heard about my father?" — as if she is in search of his killers, of the one who might have that one eye. Tellingly, the question being answered is "How much of yourself would you give?" Yet the comfort lies in the making of this poem, this list that could be mistaken for a suicide note, and beyond that, the persistence of questions.

And yet, Shiferraw also finds grounding and comfort in a very gendered sense of history and place. Women offer her answers to questions, and women offer her a way to understand the world. Yet we encounter a feminist sensibility that boldly eclipses the stereotypes of femininity. In "Twenty Questions for Your Mother," the mother's response to the question, "Tell me about your daughters" positions the woman as a figure who inherits roles and positions that have often been granted only to men:

> This is what I tell them —
> you are not women, or children
> you are kings among men
> and kings excel at what they do
> and kings do not cry
> they do not bend
> they do not run away

In "Ode to Things Torn," Shiferraw makes explicit the impulse in herself to right the ways in which women are forgotten, ways in which the woman's power is made invisible.

> you will be told
> this blood is not yours
> but the blood of your forefathers
> (foremothers? why do they always forget the mothers?)

Later in the same poem, she continues to celebrate what she defines as the feminine factor, the vital factor of the human experience — the element that, in this poem and in many others in the collection, gives value and strength to the man:

Here is the beginning of a tale:
once there was a warrior king

with the bloodline of a lion
and the heart of a woman —

Shiferraw is bold enough to title one of her poems "Being a Woman,"
and while it does not attempt to contain all that she wants to say about her
womanness — since she clearly explores this idea in so many of her other
poems — in this one, she allows herself to celebrate the complexity of her
womanhood. "I am a woman," she says, "and nothing more." The poem,
though, ends with a disturbing realization — the realization she admits she
has spent time trying to avoid, but one that she must face:

And the beauty of the night reminds me of that danger,
and muffled words, and facial hair and

heavy aftershave, and baggy pants and the sides of freeways
there! Symbols of what I could become, if only I weren't

a woman, to be raped in broad daylight and be
apologetic about it. If only I knew. But sometimes

I forget.

And it is in this that we find one of the most alluring and arresting
strengths of Shiferraw's poems — her vulnerability and the resultant boldness
to speak of it. In a sequence of seven poems ("Being a Woman," "Rumors,"
"Visitor," "Broken Men," "Song of the Dead," "Awakening," and "Statues")
near the end of the collection, Shiferraw introduces two important tropes
that speak directly to her writing of gender. The first is that of the second
self — a kind of double personality that is defined by fantasy — a psychic
bifurcation that she feels compelled to make in order to survive trauma.
So in poems like "Rumors" and "Visitor" she speaks of this other self — one

that she can rescue from men who attempt to assault and rape her, and one that may rescue her from her own internalized anxieties of self. In "Statues" she has begun to speak directly to this self—she becomes the "you," a fully realized identity:

> Put a restraint
> on yourself, and self-pity
> like the one you had
> for the crippled spider
> making its way slowly, up your legs
> to your crippled thighs;
>
> tell yourself
> there is much to be gained
> from stillness
>
> playing dead, *being dead*
>
> imagining yourself farther away,
>
> motionless;
>
> even statues
> breathe out a little
> when violated
>
> a pugnacious exhale
> released, then quickly absorbed
> into thick fog.

She is now giving direction to the traumatized self, a self that was unable to fight back, to resist, a self that could allow the body to be invaded, a self that pitied the "crippled spider" who happens to be, in many ways, the figure of a ghost or the dead or of the broken men. The advice is, of course, troubling—it demands silence, a kind of disappearance, but it constitutes exactly that kind of disappearance that the poems themselves resist and undermine. This split self, of course, is manifested in other ways. In moments, the self is the memory of someone else who stays alive by becoming that second self. And in her poems, that self is again a "you," a quite specific "you" with whom she has an engaged conversation. Perhaps the most important of such figures of memory is Abahagoy, whom she addresses in "Dear Abahagoy—." Through this character, Shiferraw is able to describe the core sensibility of her family as storytellers and therefore as people who sustain themselves through the telling of stories. In an important way, Abahagoy becomes, for Shiferraw, something of a muse, except that in this instance, the relationship with the muse is complicated by that fact that her unwillingness to invoke this voice comes from her unwillingness to contend with the death of the owner of the voice. In the end, however, Abahagoy gives Shiferraw a reason to write:

> it takes a while to absorb your voice
> and etch it into every rock, every tree, every glass blade,
> into the vast blue sky
> into milk containers and dove feathers
>
> I would've etched it into every room's wall
> every house
> every foreign land I stepped into
>
> then I wouldn't be so afraid
> because your voice will guide me
> through it all
>
> because everywhere I go
> it would be home,
>
> *it must be home*
> *because of you.*

The second trope is one to which we are introduced in earlier poems, but it begins to assume a pathology, which, like the splitting of selves, becomes a source of understanding and potential healing. In this instance, it is her fascination with ghosts, with shadows, which she treats as similar to, if not interchangeable with, memory and imagination. Of course, this ghost is not the same as the one she meets in Abahagoy, who, as I have argued, represents a kind of second self. Here the ghosts are typically male and, in many ways, antagonists: "I'm in love with the dead / because they don't talk," she says in "Song of the Dead." This is an ironic statement, as the rest of the poem, and the many other poems in the collection, all point to the fact that her relationship with the dead is hardly characterized by silence. On the matter of the talking dead, she adds:

Sometimes they do
but merely through night whispers
when I need them the most.

She welcomes these whispers, but even when thinking of the past, she constructs the haunting and traumatic relationships as those she has developed and continues to experience with the dead. In "Broken Men" she writes a touching confession that turns what has become the common warning given to women who seek to "fix" their men into a lyric justification of why this act of trying to revive, even rescue these "broken men" can have its own appeal. She knows, ultimately, that these men, who are abusive in their adult state, are essentially longing to return to a past "where / once they were kings."

Gender, then, is not dismissed or disappeared in these poems. Shiferraw is fully aware of the history of gender and the ways in which rituals, traditions, and a long history of humans working through their differences have come to construct a way to understand gender. For her, the mother is a creator, a figure that carries all the elements of her offspring, whether they are male or female, and in Shiferraw's mythology, which she engages with irony and a quirky kind of humor, she, as woman, both empathizes with and becomes a kind of Adam. Even as the myth of Adam has a ring of the familiar, the orthodox, we discover that by locating in the male the capacity for a feminine self, she is actually rescuing the male:

> This is a story
> about how Adam fell in love
> with himself, and part of himself
> in the shape of a woman
> and named her
> as his own
>
> just like God had named him
> as His own.
> ("Plot Line")

Shiferraw's *Fuchsia* is the third winner of the Sillerman First Book Prize, and she brings to this series a complex and elegant engagement with the self and with the idea of Africa. And in so doing, she reminds us of just how varied and exciting the poetry emerging from Africa is. Above anything else, the best of that work eschews the overgeneralized notion of Africa and Africanness. Instead it locates its meaning and power in the lyric engagement with the specific spaces of Africa that alert the poet's peculiar imagination.

Cutting through this collection is the hyena. The hyena may well be the defining symbol in this work, one that contains all the elements of strength, danger, resilience, a fierce relationship with human beings, and the capacity to survive. The hyena's yellow and brown are colors that we see repeated throughout the collection. There is something delightful about tracking the hyena through these poems. I have chosen not to spoil this experience for you. What I can say is that at each spotting of the creature, your respect and admiration for Mahtem Shiferraw will grow, for these sightings will reveal the sophistication of her poems, and above all, the care and skill with which she has organized these poems into a coherent and powerful whole that is, ultimately, a salute to memory and its uses:

> Yellow is crying; it's a bell, a cathedral in Asmara? A school? Or the shriek of a mass funeral. Yellow is dead. But listen to black. Listen to black notes, black heart, listen. Black is art. Not of the artist, the art of being. The painful art of memory. Here's to remembering.
> ("Synesthesia")

ACKNOWLEDGMENTS

Many thanks to the editors of the following literary magazines where some of these poems appeared: *Callaloo: A Journal of African Diaspora Arts and Letters*, *Blood Lotus Literary Journal*, *The Bitter Oleander Press*, *Blast Furnace Literary Journal*, *Mad Hatters' Review*, *Bohemian Pupil Press*, *Cactus Heart Press*, *The Missing Slate*, *Mandala Literary Journal*, *Luna Luna Magazine*, *Blackberry: A Magazine*, *Diverse Voices Quarterly*, *The 2River View*.

My deepest gratitude to my family for their love and support, my VCFA fellows and friends; thank you immensely to Kwame Dawes, Matthew Shenoda, Chris Abani, Gabeba Baderoon, John Keene, Bernardine Evaristo, the African Poetry Book Fund, the University of Nebraska Press and all its hardworking creative minds. Thank you to my early mentors, Sgroi Libertá and Stefano Bonizzato; my gratitude to Gail Wronsky, David Wojahn, Jen Bervin, Jody Gladding, Natasha Sajé, and Yusef Komunyakaa for their guidance and inspiration, for their unbridled support and encouragement. I am greatly indebted to those who came before me and paved the path for a small poet to be heard in this landscape. Finally, thank you to my God, always my light, even in sorrow.

FUCHSIA

Fuchsia

It's a deep purple thought;
once it unraveled prematurely
and its tail broke, leaving a faint trail
of rummaging words.

*

When I was little, growing up
in Addis Ababa, my father bought
the fattest sheep from street vendors
for the holidays. He would

pull its curled horns, part the wet
rubber lips to check the sharpness
of its teeth, grab its tail, separate

hairs in the thick bed of fur. Later, he will
bring it home, unsuspecting creature,
tie it to a pole in the garden, feed it the greenest
grass until its sides are swollen and heavy. It will be
slaughtered in the living room, kitchen knife

cutting in a precise angle through its neck,
the blood splattered on the blades of grass gently laid
by my mother on the cement floor, one last
comfort before its end. Come afternoon, it will
hang upside down, viscous wet smell emanating

from its insides, and knife slashing between slabs of organs,
all to be eaten differently—bones of the rib cage

deep fried, bleeding texture of kidneys minced
into bite-sized shapes and soaked in onion and pepper oil,
small blades of the stomach dutifully cut into long
strips and mashed with spiced butter and *berbere*. Even
the skin, bloodying fur, will be sold to passing vendors,
its head given away to neighbors who will use it for soup.

*

In September, the street shoulders of Addis Ababa
flood with yellow daisies, creating patches of sunlight
in rainy days. But every so often, a mulberry daisy
is spotted, its head barbarous in a field of gold,
dirty purple in its becoming.

The first time I saw a plum, it was lying in a pool
of swollen mangoes and papayas at a local grocery store,
and I held it in my hand, wanting to pierce the luminous
nakedness of the skin with my nails and teeth.

*

If you ask how to say "burgundy" in Tigrinya, you will be told
it's the color of sheep blood, without the musty smell
of death attached to it. It's also the color of my hair, dipped
in fire. And the greasy texture of clotted arteries, and the folding
skin of pineapple lilies, and the sagging insides of decaying roses,
and the butterfly leaves of blooming perennials, and spongy
strawberries drowning in wine.

*

Right before dusk, when the skies are incised with a depression
of shades, oranges escaping from one end into the mouth of the horizon,

freckled clouds unclog suddenly, giving shape to the pelvis
of the sky, its sheep blood visible only for a second, then bursting
into flames of golden shadows. In days like these, when
the sun's tears are fat and swollen, descending obliquely into the city,
we say somewhere a hyena is giving birth, and perhaps it is.

And then, you ask, what is fuchsia — and there's a faint smile,
a sudden remembrance, an afterthought in hiding, forgotten smells
of wildflowers and days spent in hiding, in disarray. And mulberry
daisies carried by phosphorescent winds into the warm skin of sleeping
bodies; moments spent between here and there, pockets of emptiness —
without sound, without reckoning.

*

Origins & Intersections

East Africa, AD 1100

>*Dar al salam.* The al najashi, al negusi.
>Son of the king. Another king? Or a prince?
>The fragranced cities of
>>Kilwa and Zelia.

>Mogadishu in full havoc, al moqaddasi at court.
>Pagan marketplaces,
>fruit vendors.

>Salt, nutmeg, cacao.
>>Salted air, chocolate coffee.

Women enfolded in vibrant narghile breaths, sweet mint tea and
red onion rings. Qadis in regal
strawberry marbles.

>Jasmine-flavored dusks, rampant winters in
>steaming diaries. Secretly married,
>death in public. Stoned. Timbuktu
>love letters, neguse neghestat.
>>King of kings.

What is that category? Beyond all kings? Not quite emperor?

The walashma torn between Islam
>>>and the other.

Sultans in lethargic years.
Black, black, black Africa.

I don't mean the people.

The relics of futuh al-habesha.
　　　Where do we come from?
　　　　　Does it really matter?

　　　　　　Braided numbers, hairs, alphabets.
　　　　　　　Circumcised wisdom.

　　　　　　　Salaam aleikum.

E is for Eden

It lasts a while. The bitter aftertaste of sorrow
and something sweet. Like honey waves soaked

in lemon juice, it creates hollow spaces between
moments of unabridged whiteness. Glance over

once and the skies have a different story to tell.

You were created with a purpose:

a land of all lands, neither heaven nor earth
suspended between the blue wings of oceans
and their unoccupied gaze.

Once there were creatures here, inhabiting
your luscious corners, and they prodded and swiveled
and flew to please you.

You were made in somebody's image,
but you have forgotten.

What remains now is the aftermath —
even that stripped of all its glory.

The eyes of men are saddened by the sudden
shadows unveiling in women's eyes. Your breath

was once dirt, ash, tangible, and ugly. Your face
did not exist. The contours that shape your smile,

your hairline, the timid dimple on the left cheek, they
were all ash. Here is what was: only the thought of

being loved and rejected, being loved and birthed,
being loved and destroyed. Your breath does not have

the apple's acrid taste; it smells of something wild and
unadorned, it says do not fear, it is I, it whispers at night

when you are cold and shivering and alone in this world.

This breath is not yours to take:
mend it and oceans will flow once again.

How to Peel Cactus Fruit

Abayey used to pick the fruit
bloodied and plump, thorns
sticking out between her fingers
and squeeze it into fat drops
in a glass bowl. Then spoonful

of cold shoved down the throat.
Sometimes it softened the heat
created after the soreness of a
long, silent cry.

The fruit comes inside handwoven baskets,
in a cluttered circle, thorns of one poking blood-juice
from the other.

If you stab your teeth in, it tastes like
honey and caramelized autumn leaves; its
meat a little window into light.

This is how you peel cactus fruit:

cut the small thorns adorning its coat, or snatch
them right out of the skin — some get stuck
in the bellies of fingernails, others nest in the palms. Squeeze
the body of the fruit until it is strained; its juice or meat
squirting right out, until a small pool of blood
inhabits the endless carvings in the insides
of your hands. Then, finally, sink in the teeth
with eyes closed, and the tongue suddenly
tastes seasons, winter, rain, dust, flour, cold,
and the acrid winds of Dahlak deserts.

This is what cures war:

the taste of watery fruit
in your mouth of fire.

Something Sleeps in the Mud Beds of the Nile

It has been years since we last descended
into its fiery throat — clouds of smoke rose
like white ash into limpid air, only to disappear
under the vast green blue.

There are songs for this river, love songs, mournful songs,
children's songs. They say this is where it all began, where it all
ends; pride is only a bleak version of the soapy waters
and their wet aftermath.

It is birthed beneath the hiccups of Lake Tana —

one could see its point of origin
only in clear, early mornings.

Sometimes the chants of hermit monks
can be heard from small islands, their prayers traveling
only through pebbles and washed mud,
their prayers only for more water.

At night, its voice is raucous as a wounded lion —

it breathes in and out, life, leaves, unguarded children
and lovers.

When shepherds approach it with their herds
its waters recede just a little bit, changing their shade
from snowy to gray and something translucent;

the eyes of cows reflect into another dimension.

The smell of something wild and torn, dirt and splintering,
speed and light conquers its sides, winter coarse under its
feet, safe nest for corpses, untold stories, the thirsty,
the poor, and the grief-stricken.

And beneath it all, something sleeps, damp and forgotten
and cavernous in its roar — only those who drink its swelling
waters can hear it, and recount its secrets.

Twenty Questions for Your Mother

When did you bleed for the first time?
        She will say — it was when I was holding
        the green skin of guava fruit, and its lilac
        meat. The juice squirted out so quickly
        I thought it was mine to take.

What did you notice then?
        The sky had a solitary eye
        on top of the mountain, where the horizon
        line curved itself into the redundant nature
        of tall trees; it was only noon, and yet
        a fat tear was approaching fast.

Tell me about the time you fell in love.
        I was angry. The harsh whiffs of
        desert winds and the striking hands
        of older brothers made the same sound,
        like a wave of the Red Sea was cut from its
        drooling origin and shoved into the unassuming
        whiteness of salt dunes. But words filled my
        mouth, and the taste was new, milky.

What happened to your hair?
        It was the same color of my shadow; its
        texture harrowing at night. When Mother
        was jailed, it felt her absence, her sharp tone
        and gentle eyes. It fell in mouthfuls at a time;
        it was Autumn and even leaves were falling then.

What of your sisters?

> I planted a seed for each of them, wished they
> could come earlier. I knew them before they
> were born. My cheeks bruise so their hair
> won't fall.

And your brothers?

> I loved each in separate corners of my abdomen;
> S. at the center, G. in the right, M. on the left,
> Y. spread thinly all over my body. When I think
> of Father, each of their eyes emerge from nowhere,
> and I am there again.

When armed men came, where did you hide?

> I didn't. I was taught to stand. They were looking for
> something in the dark, and I was the light. Even now,
> their footsteps can be heard right before sunrise.
> I see only morning lights.

What about your father?

> He sits on a cloud. I grieve every day.

And your mother?

> I woke up at dawn to wash clothes
> and stretch them to dry. I cleaned,
> cooked, and warmed the house. The mornings
> were so quiet I could hear my heartbeat. And
> merchants traveling from Karen. I hid behind
> open doors to read and write. She was awake.

Tell me about your friends.

>Some got lost in the fight. Some brought back
>children not their own, others were promised
>to men in silk suites and lovely pastries. We ate
>ice cream and went to the cinema. We spoke
>other languages. We rushed back home before
>curfew and never questioned the strident noise
>of bullets that came afterhours.

Who saved you?

>God was always there.

What of your children?

>I taught them how to read
>so they didn't have to hide.

What about your only son?

>He's still only a baby —
>safe in the warmth of my belly
>where armed men can't come after him
>and beautiful women can't take him away
>and spirits can't blacken his wings.

Tell me about your daughters.

>This is what I tell them —
>you are not women, or children,
>you are kings among men
>and kings excel at what they do
>and kings do not cry
>they do not bend
>they do not run away
>they do not hide
>they do not surrender.
>Kings excel even as they fall.

Where is the earth that fed you?
>I don't know. It belongs to those who
>died. I have asked many times why the earth
>keeps regurgitating me. I move away
>and a faint trail follows me home. I belong—
>and not.

What of Asmara?
>My city is dead.

How did you cry?
>In the quiet hours of the morning—
>I didn't have enough in me for
>wailing, but quiet tears find their
>way down my cheeks, birthed
>from my abdomen. They leave small
>knots there, and years later, I am unable
>to untie from myself.

Who did you kill?
>Bones are lovely during winter;
>their whiteness is tamed by corroded
>pores and something empty. I am reminded
>of Massawa, and the screams of neighbors
>as the city was bombed. The Red Sea must
>have been really bleeding then.

What did you listen to?
>A long list of names, martyr heads.
>A soundless prayer.
>The laughter of Father.

Who are you?
>I am free.

While Weeping (Broadway & 5th)

Someone whispers.   Someone greets.
This city
     drones at night, it rustles
     spitting, echoing
teasers, unyielding in
          somber swellings.
A man dressed in an Armani suit and
bare feet stumbles upon a
         squatted bum.
You must have forgotten yourself here,
      because   I have no recollection
           of the aftermath.
Something is fading from
the corners, cascading itself on
        corroded, corrupted
         walls. Weeping
          walls. Walls with
          cloudless
graffiti knifed in them.
     Somewhere, a baby
       howling. It is too cold to cry.
The doorman, the
      desk clerk, frigid as
     frosted breath emerging from
     windowpanes.
A boy wrapped in a
flag, wailing in
        flagellated
          irony.

The driveways, and
drive-throughs
                    on the oddly deflated
        sunrise.
                    A mother contemplating the
                        backbone of her son,
            reaching to flatten the
                        sluggish
air with her feathery fingers,
        there, where
                    he used to be.
                            It is   a different time now.

The Monster

(after David St. John's The Face)

The monster. The dreamer, the eater. The eater monster. You the
monster, I the monster. All of us the monster. The monster in us, the
monster in you. The monster in all of us. Us the monster, the cheater,
the weaver. The monster the cheater of life, the cheater of death, the
monster of the woman, the monster of her servant. The monster
the cheater, the monster of the tears, the tears of the monster. The
monster and the flesh, the monster with the flesh, the flesh of the
monster. The monster the eater, the monster the cheater, the monster
the servant, the monster the monster. The monster of these walls, the
walls within the monster. The monster in you, the monster in me,
the monster in us. The lover. The monster the lover, the monster the
monk. The monk and the flesh of the monster, the flesh of the monk
with the monster. The monster the eater, the monster the cheater,
the monster the servant the monster in you. The monster in here, the
monster in Sesame Street. The monster of the children, the children
in the monster, the child in the monster. The monster of money,
the monster of disease, the disease of the monster of the flesh of the
monk. The monk. The monster. The monster the eater the monster
the cheater the monster the servant the monster in you the monster
in the monk the monster the child of the child of the monster.
The monster in all of us. The monster in water, the monster of this
liposuction, the monster in LA. The monster of LA. The monster of
the flesh of LA, the monster of the child in LA, the monster of the
servant of LA. The monster. The dreamer, the weaver. The monster in
Hollywood, the monster of Hollywood, Hollywood and the monster.
A love affair. The monster and the love affair. The monster and the
flesh of the monster in a love affair. The monster in you on Venice
Beach, the monster in Culver City, the monster in here, right now,

right there, nowhere. The monster nowhere. The monster everywhere. The monster the eater, the monster the dreamer the monster the lover, the monster the flesh of the monk of the child in LA. The monster of you and the monster in me. The monster in all. The monster.

Talks about Race

I have dark skin, dark face, and darkened eyes—

the white resides only outside the pupil.

I don't know how to think of this—
I wasn't taught to notice one's colors;

under the sun, everyone's skin bounces streaks of light.

Which do I claim? It is difficult to explain
the difference between African & African American
the details escape me, thin paper folding the involucre of a burning fire.

I am "other"; it is such
an indistinguishable form, beyond the construct of the proper self.

Sometimes I am asked
if I am Indian, Middle Eastern, or Biracial;

I don't know what to say to these people
who notice the shape of the eye before its depth
the sound of the tongue before its wisdom
the openness of a palm before its reach.

And what to those who call me "African"?
Don't they know I can count the years spent back home
wishing I knew I was "African"?

And how to cradle and contain the disappointment that is
rekindled whenever someone does NOT know
my Ethiopia, my Eritrea.

I don't know how to fit, adjust myself within new boundaries —
nomads like me, have no place as home, no way of belonging.

Sleeping with Hyenas

It's like this: most moonless nights
are governed by the daunting laughter
of spotted hyenas. It's a fact.

Sometimes in groups, other times
in solitude, traveling through fields of corn
and teff, past the small forest of eucalyptus
trees and into the neighborhood. Red light

flickering behind the pupils, tongues
drowning in sticky saliva, ears bent
forward for the slight rustling of shifting
air, in movement. Their paws plundering,

barely touching the ground. Once you notice
the red flicker, there is nothingness. Only
the howling of nervous dogs, often the prey.

But mostly, hyenas:

crossing small rivers and surviving the gushing
sound of men shouting in high-pitched shrieks
for the inundating smell of forgotten flesh;
rebellious puppies, chickens out of their

nests, solitary humans lingering in dark
afterhours. The hunt is best when they travel
in small groups: hunchbacked, limping, gluttonous
masses of gray gently mapping out traps

through the repeated and nauseating motion
of circling, circling, circling, until the voracious
nails and sharp teeth suddenly find themselves on
the edge of freshly caught meat, perhaps still alive, still
bleeding. But there is one night, once a month, when

animals are at their worst; people in the
neighborhood swear it seemed like the
devil was approaching fast, its feet pounding
the earth. And the white hyena appears: slow,
majestic movements, the drizzling saliva
collected in a pool on the sides of its mouth.

It comes only for the fattest cow, or sheep, laid out
halfway through its journey, before descending
to the valleys, and it will feast on it. People peep
through window holes, consumed by the arduous

task of grief and sacrifice, trying not to think
how many men would the cow have fed
how many children would its milk have raised.

Once, I peeked through my window, suddenly
sensing its maddening laughter quieted down:

and there it was, staring back, the limp body

of our puppy sticking out from its jaws, blood
dripping with saliva.

That night, *I thought I saw it — something unnatural.*

And I slept.

She says they come at night . . .

like diligent thieves, quick and
quiet. They take things, small
small things, tuck them deep into
their pockets, roll them like socks, cup
their palms against the warm cloth
to feel certainty.

How do they know?

They lurk; each home has its own devil.
They smell: sucked air, thin air, empty air.
They probe: curved swallows, thickening fear.

I say, they must come at night.
She says they do.

I say I already hear them, their footsteps a faint
forking of carpet hairs. She says their silence
is white. But I do hear them.

She says there is no quietness in me.
I think that's a good thing.

Firstborn sons were killed on a quiet night,
like any other.

I say diligent thieves get only
what they came for.

She says they do.

The ones rattling as if they were discomforted, as if they did not belong there. Quick and quiet. Taken. Like small things. Small small things. Lolled and rolled.

Water

It all happens at night —
    I am out in the ocean
    contemplating my next suicide
and you forget to wake me

sometimes I find you
alone, exhausted
your eyes filled with emotions
you didn't know you had
counting the fish, the shells, the leafs
each drop of water
because, they too, didn't want to be
forgotten

other times
you are just a voice
a touch
a whisper of air
against my cheeks, my lungs
slowly filling with drops

a waterfall pouring laughter

rain descending, decomposing
my flesh

water is our thing, you say —
we drink until we die,
together
until we are sure
that each drop of water
is counted, called, remembered.

Polka Dot Dreams

These dreams are not real. They are not. They are not.
      See how they travel, with the kiss of a dead soul
and the lost aunt of the next-door neighbor. That boy
in the blue suit does not know who he is, and his dreams
tell him, you are the boy in the blue suit. But he changes
colors at night,
      he becomes coral Vespasian
      full of
worming jingles.

But the dreams are not real. Like the mother, who dreams
of vivid springs and never-ending autumns, the oranges and the
      berry browns flaking with the snow,
      she sees every shade of her
olives and grapes.

If she wakes up. She is color blind.

These dreams are not real. The polka dots are not
real. They are missing a spot, a life,
      a detangled masterpiece.

These dreams that coagulate in the old man's throat and
descend in the tumor of the liver he loves so much. He was thinking
of donating his, why not? But he cannot, he cannot. So, be careful
with these dreams, they are not real, but they are not here, they're
just in motion, they travel between the tumor and the coral lines
of midnight flavors,
      they quarrel with white hyenas and storming
bee queens. These dreams are not real. They are not.
      They are not. See? They travel,

they still travel and lurch of dead souls,
and blue corals and viscid
leaves and empty dots and vapid livers and
drunken bees and hyenas.

These dreams are not real.
They are not.
They are not.
You are not.

Blood Disparities

My sister — not the weird artist who
drew me with a hammer soaring over
my forehead — but the one who's trying to become
a doctor — she said that understanding biology and chemistry
will help me understand lives, and perhaps save them;

she said, if I looked at the intimacy shared between the
small and large intestines, crawling comfortably with each
other in sprawling heated caves, I would understand
what it meant to be together and alone at the same time;

she said, if I witnessed autopsies of lab cats, murdered rats
I would understand the devotion and dedication
of red blood cells, scurrying and flinching to sink into
our veins, or if I fathomed the duplicity of the different colors
of blood — raspberry blood, strawberry blood,
teething gums blood, bloody hell blood — I could make poetry
and conceive words, like anaphylaxis, and $C_6H_{12}O_6$

pretending to understand concocted, warped lives, when all
I can see is the flesh, and the wound within the flesh,
and the salmon blood, and the chestnut crust, and the dead —

Synesthesia

White is a color,
black is art. Nod to those before you.
Brown is a sense of being, and dark hovers
only beneath the shadows of necks —
those who fear it most. Here is to fear.

Red are the tips of shoes of the woman
who waited in the bathroom patiently when I was
only three — to steal my mother's ruby earrings. White

is the unsafe silence of bathroom walls, and their
morbidly cubic nature. White is water running under
my feet, the innocent screams of schoolchildren
at lunch hour.

Brown is the anomalous texture of curtains from my
childhood. Brown is also the parched wood
of a small coffee grinder my mother used. Brown as in
the intimate angles of sharply cut *ambasha* my grandmother
made, flour and water, lemon skin and cinnamon shreds, the
dark heads of raisins, while on a cargo plane back to Ethiopia,
the tired eyes of war victims and their slow recovery. Brown
is also the color of my skin, but I didn't know it then.

Blue are the waters embedded in my grandmother's eyes. Blue is
the whisper of the Nile, *Abbay*. Blue is the color of the brave. Blue
are the walls of empty neighbors' houses and the insides of their
living rooms. Blue is skimmed milk tearing the sky.

White sometimes comes back at odd hours. White are stranger's eyes drenched in sadness. White is the uniform of doctors, the smell of alcohol and something mad. White is absence. Purple comes back

as shoes, American shoes. Sky and blood under a quiet shadow. The shadow of a young tree planted in memory of a murdered teacher in high school. And the milky paste of overripe figs spurting prematurely, spiking insides. Purple is warmth in mid-July, when rain hails on corrugated tin roofs and the leaning green arms of lonely corn plants.

Yellow is crying; it's a bell, a cathedral in Asmara? A school? Or the shriek of a mass funeral. Yellow is dead. But listen to black. Listen to black notes, black heart, listen. Black is art. Not of the artist, the art of being. The painful art of memory. Here's to remembering.

Listro (Shoe-Shiner)

Brush, black shoes,
brown shoes,
brush.

Mother is sick.
No injera at home.
Sara was raped.
Father, drunk.

Shred the towel
for the white shoes.

Rip off your notebooks
        (brush!)
school won't heal
Mother. No detergent:
spit! It'll do.

Brush until
you see yourself
staring back.
For a *santim* more.
Brush.

One day
You'll have shoes too.

Brush.

Pilgrimage to the Nile

Look at the life
that someone else leads
in a land where men are free to mourn
as they please;

      look at what descends before dawn
footprints sinking into dancing quicksand
the hollow whistling of wind and its loving
touch when it reaches the sharp edges of mountaintops;

      look at the different colors of light
and the strange way shadows travel from one
end to another, and
      papers glaciers melting as if
they were engulfed by the tongue of the earth —

there in its deepest pockets, shakes and
distills dirt from crystalline mirrors and the muddy
beds of rivers;

      look at what happens when
the knot of an idea
unfolds beneath your eyes;

you are someone, anyone, in a story, a life,
sleeping like corpses do on the sides of the Blue Nile
and perhaps you were meant to be a king
and you didn't know it; or you were sold as a lover

or you were the secret keeper of your tribe
and you walked so far away from home, only to find out,

that mountains have the same heads everywhere, and they hide
hunter owls in their valleys, and acacias grow only
where the view is the loveliest, the sand the softest,

and you can crush cactus tubes and suck the sweet water out —
not because of despair, but because
you've always wanted to do that — live on the
brink of the edge
as if you were someone else.

Dinner with Uncles

We have heard these stories many times before —

how starving guerilla fighters looked out for each other
in a time where the cause was greater than human life.

Like the story about Uncle Ghirmay and his unit;
having starved for days at a time, with only boiled

water from silvery streams and the muttering taste of
Massawa salts for dinner, waiting by the feet of angry valleys.

Or the story of Uncle Silay, thought to be dead,
and one day finding himself beyond the village of

Gejeret, finding a woman that resembled a lot
his mother selling eggs and baked *kiccia* — a mother

who traveled a long way pretending to be a vendor just
to see the breathing eyes of her firstborn son.

And then there's the story of Uncle Eyob, who was lost
in Saudi Arabia for years, but hid in our house rooftop day

and night, eating whatever Asmeret cooked for us, being
stubborn as only teenage boys can be. Once, enemy

soldiers came looking for him, and he must have been
so quiet, so breathless, we really thought he was gone.

But there's a story, I hear, once in a while, from a relative,
a stranger, a distant cousin, perhaps one of the uncles —

And the story goes:

there used to be a hyena, dry of laughter, scared and squeamish
from spearing bullets splitting the hollow air and dusty winds traveling

from islands of Dahlak. Once, it dragged itself across a river or stream,
barely surviving, following the yearned smell of human flesh

and fleeting small reptiles. They say it found its way to an improvised
camp of young rebels, some wounded, some aghast from strenuous

fighting, arched backs and the luminous splendor of *zahr* adorning
their bony neck-hallows, huddled around a fire, without smiles, or words.

And it is said, that the hungry hyena fulfilled its long wish
of tasting human flesh, when it was finally found, tired salivating eyes

and molten tongue, and was secretly chopped into pieces and its red
meat was sunk into hot boiling soup. Later, thinking of wounded

rebels eating soup in silence, I wondered if they felt it —
the taste of flesh on flesh, reviving them into ravaged war.

In the Lion's Den

A stone was brought and placed
over the mouth of the den. A stone

it was, to keep me inside, to awaken
my fears — such hopelessness. And

there they stood: three heads, beds
of fur and quiet paws. Their eyes were glass

and moist, their rib cages jabbing the golden skin.

I am only a man

and do best what men do most:
fear, and loathe, and hide.

Jaws opened one by one:
breaths filled with saliva
sour taste of unkempt shadows
lurking from angular sharp teeth,
tongues dangling with strawberry insides.

What I smelled most:

their hunger, staunching of despair
and something gray. I want to open my
mouth and tell them something, anything —
speak as if I have any authority upon
myself.

What they smell at once:

the dissipating scent of something cold
and unadorned, gathering itself into small
pockets of glossy sweat, liquids flowing as if

I was an animal; and I am.

It is not my doubt, or dread coating my skin —
suddenly inviting, and the flesh, a hint of raspberry —
that overwhelms. It is a veil, thin-threaded, swirling,
filling empty corners, and the naked spaces between
their paws as they saunter slowly, dust unfettered
under the soft touch.
And suddenly there I am:

my fingers uncrossing under layers of fur,
a tingling sensation — a mixture of warmth
and the wet aftermath of a familiar lick.

Where I am — it is home;

in the lion's den.

Daisies & Death

(Koki's painting)

Death approaches with fresh daisies,
serene as a clueless sky. If you take a closer look,
faces will emerge, swollen like stung tokens,
shredded in sugared specks and fragments,
bundled up like ivory turnips, swaying from side
to side, distorting their bodies with your pupils,
and, finally, disgorged by other faces.

*

Once a little girl, now an uncomplicated
squalor plastered on a lacerated sky.
It is not dark, but the absence of light
croaks fervidly in translucent infestation,
swamping in azurite spurts from her sides,
(spattered all over her lower body)
whisking with maroon streaks of blood.

*

If I were the artist, which I am not, which I could be,
I would not tell you to get over it. You can preach
about AIDS to the world, but daisies don't even smell good.

Something Familiar and Freezing

The truth
is never what it seems;
and yet —
it breathes into our eyes.

The nights hide
cold shadows and
something white.

The green skins of cactus fruit,
rosy seeds of guava heads and
burnt bruises on tomato cheeks.

This is what you should remember —

the taste of something familiar
and freezing.

Your uncles are lost;
some at sea, crossing
the unforgiving dunes of young deserts,
others already on the mountains of Jubba.

Remember this uncle; remember
his face, the way his hairline recedes
just a bit deeper in the napes of his
eyes, the way he smiles at the sun.
Look at the face; now, forget the name.

If they ask, he was not here, in hiding
in fear, he did not escape without
a note to his mother. He did not exist.

That is what you must remember.

A Dead Man's List

The disturbance of a calm
surface of water, stagnant in its poise,
clueless really.

The way Jess's boxes
are assembled neatly
by her bed.

The smell of lavender
unfolding
beneath shadows.

The rumbling of skies
falling ghostly to the ground
as if they owned
the earth, the soil,
the dirt.

The rustling
of objects within
objects,
barely breathing.

Warmth of light,
flickering
of familiar eyes.

And the way
tears resurface, slowly,

heavily
droplets gathered from skin
beneath skin

finally erupting.

Dialectics of Death

*

WHEN WOULD YOU LIKE
TO DIE?

Gail says
she bought the plot
a long time ago —
not when she found out
her illness, which didn't
quite change things, but which did somehow —
but when she fell in love.

Here, dear, she said, here
is where we'll be, in a few years,
and that if we're lucky, lying
skull to skull, our bony fingers
carving the soil. Our teeth will
look terrible.

He says, I am sure your
hair will fall first.

Here, my love, my hair
your hair.

*

IT IS A SIMPLE QUESTION.
Esmeralda unties her shoes
one more time, knotting
gray strings
over and over again.

She says
it's not as complicated
as you think.

I will trip on these knots,
fall off the bridge,
get hit by a car.

I say,
I brought you bleach.

*

IF YOU KNEW, WOULD YOU HIDE?
IF YOU DIDN'T, WOULD YOU WORRY?
Marlena wants to be a boy.
She says the little girl in her
died; she can't recall when.

She will come back home
as Marlon.

Her father won't understand.

*

WOULD YOU CHOOSE HOW?
There are so many different
ways to do it.

Margo handles her clientele
professionally. She lights a
cigarette, blows circles of winds,
unfrolicks her hair.

The pill, of course.

—Lipstick-smeared whispers—

And the pillow.

She lights another, furious gestures.

The wrists, I remind her.
And tall buildings.

Too bloody.
Too messy.

What if I survive, both?

Yes, what if?

*

OLD AGE, GREAT ILLNESS, TO DIE
IN YOUR SLEEP?
It's a Tuesday night.
A tall dark-haired man
sits on a soggy couch, his
shoulders arched, nostrils
flickering at every breath.

His wife approaches quietly,
kitchen knife in one hand
cross in the other.

You see this vein, she says,
*this blue one, popping out
from his skin?*

That's mine.

WOULD YOU STILL LOVE?

> I dated a boy once
> who thought he was death.

> He wore black capes, dark makeup,
> butt-cracking jeans. He spoke of
> the afterworld, the damned, the just.
> He ate bloody meat and fresh guts,
> warm still. He called me darling.

> Darling, look into my eyes.
> What do you see?
> Do you see death?

> Because that is how
> it must look like.

> Not white light,
> then absence.

> *Yes, I see it, now.*

HOW MUCH OF YOURSELF
WOULD YOU GIVE?

> Mayumi wants to know
> who killed her father, like that,
> like an animal, who hanged him
> upside down from the sycamore,
> who lacerated his back, who took
> one eye, and left the other, solitary,
> by itself.

She wants to know
if the leaves swallowed his last
words, if the winds softened his
pain, if the earth drank his blood.

All she has to do
is smell your fear:
have you heard something, dear?

Have you heard about my father?
Have *you* heard about my father?

And she will know. If you have.
She will know if you have that eye.

*

WOULD YOU STILL HAVE
THE COURAGE TO WAKE
EVERY MORNING?

Angelique likes to sleep;

she lays supine, her skin
opening up like warm tulips
her feet tracing cold walls
her heartbeat softened by
the night.

Though Mondays are quite different.

That's when she sprawls on her side;
legs lifted up to her chin
palms cupped as if in prayer
eyes wide open to adjust to darkness.

That is how she wants to die,
womb to womb.

Though she dies a little
each night.

*

WOULD YOU
RATHER NOT?

What would be my last thought?

Would I think of you? Or would
I think of the last thing I started but
didn't finish?

Would it matter that I had this list,
this long list of people
I wanted to kill, or love
before I died?

Would they think it was a
suicide note or a sweet good-bye?

Would I die again?
Would I love a ghost again?

*

Being a Woman

Sometimes I forget. I become a volatile spirit
a butterfly out of its wings, a blooming flower

in decay. I fall in love with ghosts and cry
when they flesh out, brains interwoven like baskets.

I squeal like sometimes birds do, and words
fail to rise to my mouth. I trade shapes with

dancing shadows, untangle hand-painted walls, sink
in discomforted glares crazing through the night.
But at times I am reminded;

a slow, agonizing awakening piercing through my being
sharp as cut glass, and it curls and whirls until I am fully

awakened. It brings the faint smell of freshly picked lilacs,
the trace of oily fingers left on windowpanes, shaved heads

bulging from the crowds — all there to remind me that

I am a woman
and nothing more.

A woman

not aware of what her womanhood might do to others, watching.

And the beauty of the night reminds me of that danger,
and muffled words, and facial hair and

heavy aftershave, and baggy pants and the sides of freeways
there! Symbols of what I could become, if only I weren't

a woman, to be raped in broad daylight and be
apologetic about it. If only I knew. But sometimes

I forget.

Rumors

I've recently heard rumors about this
    other self I am possessed with, and I
      wonder, what does she

    look like? Does she have my same braided
      hair? Does she walk like I do, slight slant
to the right foot, quickening steps? And

    does she curl up in the dark, as if erupting
out of the womb?

      Is she sitting at
          the far corner of a café, writing in my journal,
        sipping my favorite latte? She is not timid,

she does not cover her eyes, and her palms
    aren't sweaty. She is the strong one of us.
      But what

    will she do when I am not there, and we
      are both assaulted? When it happened, I froze, my veins
        suddenly frigid. But she would run away, and
      weep; she'll keep us safe. What if she

doesn't make it, out of this, out of me? What
    if I am the only one to resurface, day after day,
      would she die of drowning? Or would she be
me again? I've heard rumors, about this other

    self,

and I can't help but wonder how long it
would take for us to see what the best thing
is for me, to stay like this, split, unnumbered,

or to awaken, surreptitiously birthed.

Visitor

Every night, I wait for you.
The unsophisticated version of you,
when I least expect it. You walk in

through closed doors, like a ghost,
a pale presence barely there. I do not
know who you are, but I suspect
you have been here before;

and I must have been weaker then, to let you
in so soon after losing myself. I tuck in

the handcrafted knife under the pillow, feel its
metallic coolness on my burning skin. This is not
the first time I have thought of you, and you

materialize within walls. Your image, the shadow
of my unwanted thoughts.

I know how this night is going to end. I will breathe
so heavily until that is the only sound I can hear. You
just want this to be over, as always; perhaps you have
somewhere else to be? I quiver and pull the covers up high,

but nothing protects me from your gelid touch. I cannot
see your eyes. I would be betraying myself.

I only feel the touch, now familiar, mechanic, rigid. You almost
feel sorry for me. I think I won't let you in next time.

Broken Men

I'm interested in them
because they take years to mend.

I can gather their pieces
one by one
scattered in street corners
and parking lots —

I can trace back their thoughts
there, where they left them

at the Chinese Laundry strip club
on Rodeo and La Cienega
hoping for a pitiful lap dance;

I can find them
when they were just teenagers
hiking the upper decks of malls
to catch a glimpse of women's breasts

or when they were ten
and tried to cover up their ears from

the thumping
father hitting mother
and her silence

I can see them reading in the dark
with the fickle light of

a draping loose moon, delving
into stories better than theirs.

And I can let them into the secret —

women have eyes between
their breasts,

and they don't want you to see them.
Whenever you stare

something grows from underneath,
a sudden urge to undress
in front of a stranger, and remain
without sin, without knowing —

they want to go back where
once they were kings

and made of palpitating mud
and spit, and whispered air.

Song of the Dead

I'm in love with the dead
because they don't talk.

Sometimes they do
but merely through night whispers
when I need them the most.

At times they move slowly,

like the dance of newborns
fleshing out of the womb.

They dance because
they have nothing else to do.

But I want to think
they're here for me —
they are my audience:

before dawn
I leave water and bread
outside windows
where thin curtains flutter
flattered by such exotic dance —

such unearthly beauty — uncertain,
new, full of mud and worms

the teeth and bones
tickling each other, oh the song
of wonders! One must have ears

and so much grief to hear them.

Awakening

after Ralph Angel

As if all of this never happened
we woke up dead. It is not a dream, the
unknotted vine that crumbles at our
feet. Rather, the poisonous, exquisite
glare steaming from the window frames

so frightfully detached from their paints.
And when we lie beneath each other,
our hands a cupped vein, so perfectly abrupt
from the parching skin, we are accomplices

to the gruesome details that resurface
from the glistening barbed romance of the
porcelain dolls. Only one pupil, only one

storm to unhitch, it seems. The sandals,
the rosewater lotion canister,
your wet crimped hair. It is unsettling
how we can still dream of one another, and smile;

so much left to do, so much fatigue to
enliven, embitter

and yet, as if all of this never happened,
we woke up dead.

Statues

after Gail Wronsky

This is how you must feel
when you are stuck

in between;

the voices—so many!—
lurking like snakes in the shadows
enveloped in your skin,

corroding
as they slide by

it is unpleasant

to know
to be suspended
tucked within

perhaps you thought
you were an illusion too
just like everything else

just like they said
you would become

like a leaf left unfettered into becoming; being—

it is too much to bear.

Put a restraint
on yourself, and self-pity
like the one you had
for the crippled spider
making its way slowly, up your legs
to your crippled thighs;

tell yourself
there is much to be gained
from stillness

playing dead, *being dead*

imagining yourself farther away,

motionless;

even statues
breathe out a little
when violated

a pugnacious exhale
released, then quickly absorbed
into thick fog.

Kalashnikovs

I was only seven
the first time I heard its rumble —
quick, and sharp, in hollow air
bundling one by one
those still out after curfew.
Wrecks of buildings
and the streets of Asmara
sagging,

the people in Godaif
hid behind closed doors
and carved small holes through walls
to see whose son had died.

It was forbidden
to mourn in public.

Years later
I attend fund-raising campaigns
for Africa, thinking I can help
if only I could hear their stories.
Genocides. Sex slaves. Child soldiers.
Dictators sprouting every year with a new
ideology handing it out left and right.

Even now, at night, in this
polluted air, the beauty of a momentary silence,
between fireworks shooting to the sky
and the laughter of teenage boys in

hoodies and wool caps, I jump up,
part the curtains and peek outside, to see
if somebody's son has lost his life
to the glorious monster.

The Language of Hair

When I was twelve
I looked after Absara,
my newborn cousin with pearl eyes
and thin gold chains wrapped around
her neck and fingers.

I stared at her
until she fell asleep
then rested my head next to hers
to feel the warmth
of a dreamless world.

In our sleep, small lice travel
from my corn rolls
to her soft hairs.

Later, Ezey will yell
and stare at me until I cry.
She'll bring a cup filled with alcohol
some cotton balls
and stroke vehemently the skin, the hair
picking lice one by one
crushing their little bodies
with her thumb.

*

My mother used to spend her Sundays
braiding our hair, mine and my sisters' —

it took her all day to undo the old ones
comb them out, wait for us to stop growling
or crying—then start braiding all over again.

I liked the individual braids that fall naturally on your back;
begin measuring down the nose, spilt the hair exactly
where the eyes meet, bundle up a thin layer to build
shapes and forms you studied at school.

This is our way of being creative;

a language only women
can speak.

*

Since I came to LA, which was not that long ago,
I've managed to cut my hair in a fro, dye it orange
contemplated getting tattooed in between its bushes
got it permed and cut bangs so I can hide my eyes
added blonde polyester hair so I can pass for American
then changed it into streaks of deep purple and metallic blue
to match my nail polish, and finally grew it out
only to see it fall again.

*

Now I stay up, late at night
and braid it
because I cannot speak that language.

Small Tragedies

Everybody has a story
about how they didn't fit
        until they do—
and they want to tell it.

Here is how it begins;
how you make monsters out of children
by telling them stories
about this other world, a world where
they sink in clouds and color the earth
where forests of blue lakes
give birth to strange animals
where adults
are only a bleak version of themselves

where stories
    are never only stories.

This is how children are made;

    without intention or precision
where orange doors and glass portals
lead to another dimension,
another self.

Look at them command in this other world;
they don't hesitate, or quarrel, and they are not afraid—

they climb trees, and pick up leaves, and speak a language
made of wild berries and honey nut combs—

they grow tall, and feed off the earth and drink
its glazed colors, and swim through all shades of green —

sodden green, lime green, bruised green, emerald eyes, muddy greens
of bed waters, the blue-green of newborns laughing.

This is how
monsters are made —

    they fit
        until they don't.

4AM

4AM and the muezzin begins his chant.
Someone bows down in a silent prayer,
others whisper words swallowed into darkness.

4AM and I am still not asleep, and I draw lines
into words through breath-filled windowpanes.
Even dogs are quiet, only the rustling of acacias
shivering in the wind. Same as any other night.

4AM and the icy pupils of a white hyena sparkle
through sharp grass blades. It takes shape suddenly
sensing uneaten puppies sleeping next door.

4AM and I wonder if the moonlight is brighter
from Entoto's sky. Once I pointed a telescope
from its peak into the infinite vastness of the
Milky Way, and couldn't find answers.

4AM and muffled words break the silence, the earth
beneath me suddenly shaking, the gentle click-clack
of rifles against warm cloth. I am just a child lost
in a world where hyenas bewitch with nervous laughter.

4AM and men in uniforms rush through our small house
made of *chikka* and battered cement, through the narrow
red corridor and into my parents' bedroom.

The muezzin's voice seems so far away, now. I should've bowed
in prayer, it should've been my words swallowed back into
darkness. But I am only a child, and do not know where
guns belong. Or the sodden hearts of those who carry them.

Dear Abahagoy —

there is a picture of you somewhere
inside a white binder
you wear a blue suit, and I a red apron
with white polka dots

your skin is so dark, and mine so white

you wouldn't know we are related.

I am only a baby
(Is it my first birthday? My second?)

I sit on your lap
and the world is new.

Sometimes I think of you
deep into the night
worried I might forget you;

but I was young enough to remember you
and not young enough to forget the pain.

You are nowhere.

And yet here you are, bits of you
suddenly shaking our world
into nostalgia, laughter, joy;

I see your eyes in my uncles' eyes
that skin I remember, so smooth,

a luminous black, and the quick smile,
the familiar chuckle, inhabiting the strange
faces of relatives and cousins.

But what about your voice? Where do
I go to hear that?

There is light in my mother's eyes
when she thinks of you
and I'd like to think
I see a white cloud surrounding her head
and mine, when she does.

And there are stories, of course, stories
told over and over again — that time one uncle
ate all the bread, the time with the ox, the time
of the market, the time you ran out of the house
without shoes when your country was set free.

We all remember these stories
because we want to remember you;

we tell them to each other
over and over again;

it is an obsession
that does not let us grieve.

And there are pictures, of course,
and cousins with your same bravado
your same finesse, cousins with your
eyes, your mouth, your shapely farmer hands

but pictures do not speak, they do not
no matter how hard you try
no matter how loudly you address them
no matter the sorrow.

But I come from a family of storytellers
and I'd like to believe
you are still here; if not in me, then in
my mother's light, in my uncles' eyes, in my
aunts' laughter, in my grandmother's heart.

And now, look, here you are
appearing in my poem, and I can tell myself

it is okay, because this is it,

you are here
because we are.

And if I was there, when you were a young
boy, a young farmer, I would've showed you my poems
went with you to the land, asked you about our ancestors
heard your laughter get carried away with the wind
I would've sat in the dirt, safe in your presence
I would've read out loud, learned to be a poet in Tigrinya
learned to love sooner, to forgive better, to be courageous always,
to remain stubborn as I was. And I would've been quiet,
quiet as I'll ever be, because:

it takes a while to absorb your voice
and etch it into every rock, every tree, every glass blade,
into the vast blue sky
into milk containers and dove feathers

I would've etched it into every room's wall
every house
every foreign land I stepped into

then I wouldn't be so afraid
because your voice will guide me
through it all

because everywhere I go
it would be home,

it must be home
because of you.

I never told you this:

I never grieved properly for you
because that would mean
you are actually gone.

I never went back to Asmara

because what is your city without you

it is like an old photograph
in a white binder.

So here it is:
the things I wished you could see
things I wish I could tell you
so many things to show you

but mostly, I wouldn't say anything:

I would just listen
because I must not forget
your voice, your love, your grace.

And I would tell you:
dear Abahagoy
you think you are gone
because you are up there

but you are still here.

Effervescence

What dost thou, moon, in the sky? Tell me,
what are you doing, oh silent moon?

Giacomo Leopardi, XXIII from "Night Song of Wandering Shepherd"

The moon splits in half cheeks —
drooling honey and saliva.

It is something we have seen
many times before, and yet

we make up stories
to justify its velvety glow;

hear how it was spit
from the mouth of the oceans
because it could not contain itself

or how it was sliced from the heavens
when it was only a neonate
and fed wild fruits and fireflies
until its sides were bursting

the skin tightened by such
unwavering effervescence —

or the way it was born in the insides
of dark forests, unseen to wondering eyes
deep in the hungered crust of the earth
filling its vesicles in frothing glass.

We say this is what happens
to those who dare disobey, surrounded
by fierce winds sharpening the skulls of
mountaintops into loose terrains, to those

who dare question those who came
before them; to those who are awakened
suddenly by the raspy hauls of wild dogs
and the sinister laughter of spotted hyenas —

it is something we see
and fail to grasp the significance —

its cheeks are a little less fluffy
its radiance suddenly sunken

a warning to those of us
who look up to the heavens
and dare to dream.

Ode to Things Torn

Men run upstream waters
to try and catch you;

you will be told
this blood is not yours
but the blood of your forefathers
(foremothers? why do they always forget the mothers?)

it is not yours to take.

I love him
like the sun loves the moon

longing from a distance,
longing for things I did not know.

Here is the beginning of a tale:
once there was a warrior king

with the bloodline of a lion
and the heart of a woman —

where do you think this is going?

Try to assemble the wild things
before they come back
to haunt us all

before something purple
turns inside you.

A fruit is a perfect metaphor
for us, for this

but

which fruit to pick
which to leave
which to let rot
which to hide under a hairy earth?

There is a dream that begins
with rain, and morning moss, and
something torn:

it does not teach you how to mend,
how to sow, but you are given seeds
with the eyes of a thousand souls,

what will you do?

The tale goes,

the warrior king feared only but one
painting gold the houses of those he loved
those who feared him, choosing only the
firstborns for his army of soldiers

and when he looked in the eyes of the lake
there she was: the woman reflecting back
her heart in the shape of his face;

he knew then he loved her
as he loved himself

as he never dared to love himself
as she loved him.

If it rains
you can hear him weep —

his eyes emerge from wet algae and
the smooth heads of pebbles, swollen to the sun

and then you see it: the look of a man or
a woman or
a self

torn, disassembled.

Plot Line

This is a story about love.

This is a story
about how Adam fell in love
with himself, and part of himself
in the shape of a woman
and named her
as his own

just like God had named him
as His own.

This is a story
about the woman falling in love
with a stranger, a fruit, so tasty
it brought her wisdom.

This is a story
about the first tragedy
ever written.

This is a story
about you.

Adam, who told you you were naked?
      The one I love.

Adam, where are you?
      In hiding.

Adam, why do you hide?
  Because I know.
  Because I loved this part of me.

A Secret Lull

You have been given
the heart of a lion;

this is what happens
before the roar.

Think of it like this:

the moon reshapes itself
at the howls of wolves
the laughter of hyenas
the wailing of grieving widows.

Also, you can think of it as:

a childless mother's heart
drenched in sorrow and madness
(how could she not?)
whispering names for the unborn —
flower names, river names, warrior names —
and what that could be.

Sometimes when the moon is dressed
in the voices of hermit monks

something happens —

a secret lull rises to the mountaintops
and hovers beneath the shadows of oak trees
sharpening skulls into the white corpses
of eucalyptus trees. Only then one can hear

the valley of the weepers, the valley of the bones
where flowers grow thick and wild
and bear the names of a child's heart
etched in their petals.

And this is what you will be told:

warriors were once children too
and warriors had mothers
and when mothers birthed warrior children
they did not know their wombs would shut
from such grief, such brave death
they did not know
they were birthing the same sorrow
that will split them in half.

Instead, they dreamed, these mothers,
they dreamed of happy days
(how could they not?):

how the sun will bathe the small bodies
how the flesh will replace itself
the bones restructured
jawlines reaffirmed
blood thickened, veins scurrying like
streams in the valleys, eyes trained to reflect
into the unworldly.

These are the things we take for granted:

the immediate warmth of skin on skin
a kick in the second trimester
small fingers wrapping around a hand
eyes gazing always in fascination.

But the valley of the bones
is the valley of the warriors

and children are born
with the heart of a lion

and you can hear them roar
beyond the hairs of squatted trees
and wild acacias

and it is not deafening, or frightening
but a slow rumble growing from their bellies
to the corpses of flowers and mountains
past hermit monks and hyenas
and into the hearts of those yet unbirthed.

Now, who's to say
their roar's strength
does not lie in sorrow?

IN THE AFRICAN POETRY BOOK SERIES

*The Promise of Hope: New and
Selected Poems, 1964–2013*
Kofi Awoonor
Edited and with an introduction
by Kofi Anyidoho

Madman at Kilifi
Clifton Gachagua

*Seven New Generation African
Poets: A Chapbook boxed set*
Edited by Kwame Dawes and Chris Abani

Gabriel Okara: Collected Poems
Gabriel Okara
Edited and with an introduction
by Brenda Marie Osbey

The Kitchen-Dweller's Testimony
Ladan Osman

Fuchsia
Mahtem Shiferraw

To order or obtain more information on
these or other University of Nebraska
Press titles, visit nebraskapress.unl.edu.

CPSIA information can be obtained at www.ICGtesting.com
Printed in the USA
LVOW08s1842210616

493516LV00001B/219/P